REINHARD

TH
ROMANCE OF
REDEEMING
LOVE

FOUNDATION OF CHRISTIAN LIVING

CHRIST
FOR ALL NATIONS

Australia • Brazil • Canada • Czech Republic • Germany • Hong Kong • Kenya • Latin America
• New Zealand • Nigeria • Singapore • South Africa • United Kingdom • United States

THE ROMANCE OF REDEEMING LOVE

©2022 Harvester Services – Reinhard Bonnke

Published by Christ for all Nations
PO Box 590588 Orlando, FL 32859-0588
www.CfaN.org

ISBN 978-3-935057-25-7

Editor Kimberly Overcast,
Layout Oleksandr M Volyk

Printed in Colombia

FOREWORD

What are the two greatest things God ever did? The Bible tells us that He created the heavens and the earth. Could anything possibly equal that—making our wonderful world, with its oceans, mountains and rivers, and filling the heavens with stars?

In fact, God did do something else that was far more difficult. We call it the work of Redemption. Creation cost God nothing, but that next task cost Him everything.

At creation God blessed us with the energies of life. Then He blessed us with the gift of Redemption, adding new life to ordinary life. Millions of people around the world enjoy it. They are jubilant. They exclaim and sing: "I am redeemed!" They cannot keep quiet about this wonderful gift that God has given them.

Unfortunately, not everyone is alive in this way, because not everyone is redeemed. And sadly, some people have never even heard of Redemption, which is why this booklet has been written. It tells the story of Redemption for everyone who needs to hear it.

Redemption is like creation—nobody thought of it but God. It never crossed anyone's mind, not even that of the wisest person who ever lived. There are many religions in the world, but none of them offers Redemption. People believe in many different gods, but not one of them is a redeemer. There are many holy books, but only one of them brings us the good news of Redemption—the Bible.

As you read this booklet—and as you read the Bible for yourself—our prayer is that you will come to know God's Redemption for yourself. May God bless you with all the good things He longs to give you!

Reinhard Bonnke

THE
ROMANCE OF
REDEEMING
LOVE

PART 1

THE GIFT OF REDEMPTION[1]
WHAT IS REDEMPTION?

The word *Redemption* comes from *redeem*, which means "to buy back something which once belonged to you." One dictionary definition puts it like this:

Redemption: To recover possession or ownership by payment of a price. Deliverance from sin through the incarnation, sufferings and death of Christ.

To redeem something also means to obtain it by paying a ransom.

The Bible explains Redemption by using pictures or models. The greatest of its pictures is the story of how God freed the people of Israel from their slavery in Egypt. From that time on, God was known as the Redeemer. This tremendous event changed the world, but it was still only a small sketch of the great Redemption to come.

---

[1] Note: Throughout this book, *"Redemption"* appears with a capital letter *R* to signify eternal Redemption.

Alongside this great event, there are several other Bible pictures. As we look at them, they will help us to appreciate how marvelous Redemption is.

THE ISRAELITES IN EGYPT

Israel is the only nation in history that was redeemed. This was something that was achieved by God—the people of Israel did not do it themselves.

The Israelites were trapped in Egypt, and were cruelly subjected to forced labor by the Egyptians. After many years of this slavery, the Lord said: *"I will free you from being slaves to them, and I will redeem you with an outstretched arm and with mighty acts of judgment. I will take you as my own people, and I will be your God"* (Exodus 6:6–7).

And this was exactly what He did. He sent His servant Moses to the King of Egypt, with the famous instruction: "Let my people go." At first the King resisted God and refused to release the people of Israel. But eventually, after God had sent ten plagues upon the land of Egypt, the Israelites were able to escape—through the power and love of God.

This amazing event is called "the exodus"—today we might call it "the great escape"—and you can read the full story in the first few chapters of the book of Exodus.

The exodus tells us several very important things about Redemption.

God acted freely. God stepped into this desperate situation, acting entirely on His own initiative. He did not rescue His people because He had to, or because He was bound by duty. He did it freely, reclaiming what rightfully belonged to Him.

God acted for His people. The dictionary definition makes it clear that you can only redeem what you have once owned. God said that the people of Israel were His people. They belonged to Him.

God acted out of love. God redeemed the people of Israel because of His great love for them. What He did shows what He really is at heart. Just as someone might be a musician or an artist by gift and nature, so God is a loving Redeemer. As one of the Bible's prophets said: *"All mankind will know that I, the LORD, am your Savior, your Redeemer, the Mighty One of Jacob"* (Isaiah 49:26).

REDEMPTION IS FOR ALL MANKIND

The wonderful story of the exodus might make us think that Redemption was just for one particular nation at one particular time in the past. But that is not true. Redemption is much bigger than that. The truth is that all mankind needs Redemption. Redemption did not occur just once for one small race. That was like a mere demonstration! The exodus story tells us about God, and it shows us what He is like—not just what He was like then, but what He is always like, and for everybody. This is because God never changes. As we will see, He provided Redemption on a world scale and for all eternity.

The great problem on earth has always been sin. Just as the people of Israel were in slavery to their Egyptian masters, so human beings are in slavery to sin. Nobody but God Himself could possibly break its grip.

To release Israel from Egypt, God simply hurled plagues down from the heavens. But to redeem all mankind from sin, He sent His own Son from heaven. Jesus Christ is the only One who could ever truly claim to be the Redeemer. Only He could ever take on the task of Redemption. He is the Holy One, the sinless Son of God, Jesus Christ the Lord.

SEVEN FACTS ABOUT REDEMPTION

1. It is not just an idea or a subject to learn—it is something that happens to you.

2. It is not just an experience you once had—it goes on throughout your life.

3. It is not just a feeling—it is a new direction and purpose in life.

4. It is not just being good and sincere—it is becoming a new person.

5. It is not "religion", or something that you do—it is what God does.

6. It is not a human invention—it is God's business.

7. It is no credit to us—Redemption brings praise to God for eternity.

WHY DOES GOD REDEEM?

If nobody needed Redemption, God would not have sent Christ to redeem us. The French philosopher Jean-Jacques Rousseau said: "Man is born free, and everywhere he is in chains."[2] The Bible puts it like this: "The whole world is under the control of the evil one" (1 John 5:19).

The devil, described in the Bible as *the ruler of the kingdom of the air, the spirit who is now at work in those who are disobedient"* (Ephesians 2:2), has seduced everybody. There are a million temptations, urges, habits, and addictions. They drive people like the whips of the Egyptian taskmasters.

But then we read that Christ came and *"went around doing good and healing all who were under the power of the devil"* (Acts 10:38).

---

[2] Jean-Jacques Rousseau, *The Social Contract*, 1.1, SparkNotes, accessed February 23, 2022

If we come to God, we must know what He is like and what to expect of Him. If we go to the doctor, it is for medicine. If we go to a counselor, it is for good advice. So when we come to God, we come to Him as Redeemer.

What does this mean? God is a Redeemer, and so we must meet Him first for Redemption. Some treat Him as the Almighty, or as the King, or for answers to prayer, without really knowing Him. He is often gracious to them and He is, of course, the Almighty and the King of all kings, but to know Him, we must first come to Him as our Savior and our Redeemer. The first thing He wants is to save us, redeem us, and restore us to our true owner—our Maker and Father.

When this happens, we are set free. Jesus said: *"If the Son sets you free, you will be free indeed"* (John 8:36).

There are two reasons why God redeems us. First, He owns us. Second, we turned away from God and were lost to Him. Let's look at these two reasons in turn.

WE ALL BELONG TO GOD

We saw earlier that you cannot redeem what you never owned. We can see this clearly in the picture of God redeeming Israel. God was their rightful owner.

On one occasion God says: *"this people I have formed for Myself"* (Isaiah 43:21, NKJV)—and here He is talking not just about the individuals, but about the whole nation. He formed the nation Himself—providing it with His laws, His leaders, and His land. *"They are My servants,"* He said, *"whom I brought out [or redeemed] of Egypt"* (Leviticus 25:55).

Not only Israel but every person ever born once belonged to God.

The Creator owns what He creates. We have children for ourselves and so does God. The Bible expresses it in this way:

> "*The earth is the LORD's, and everything in it, the world, and all who live in it.*" (Psalm 24:1)

> "*Know that the Lord is God. It is He who made us, and we are His; we are His people, the sheep of His pasture.*" (Psalm 100:3)

The Bible also says about God: "*You created all things, and by Your will they were created and have their being*" (Revelation 4:11). All of us belong to God—and so all of us can be redeemed by Him.

A FORFEITED POSSESSION

Let's look at Israel again. They belonged to God, but they also sinned against Him. The story of the exodus tells us that they bowed down and served the Egyptian gods. Even though they did this, it did not alter the fact that God had been the God of their ancestors—and that He was still their God.

He remembered the promises He had made to the people of Israel, and this is why He told Moses: "*I have come down to rescue them from the hand of the Egyptians*" (Exodus 3:8).

Even after that history-making deliverance of the exodus, the people forgot God, but He did not forget them. In a famous passage, God says:

I reared children and brought them up, but they have rebelled against me. The ox knows it's master, the donkey it's owner's manger, but Israel does not know. (Isaiah 1:2–3)

There were times when God seemed to be on the verge of completely rejecting His people: "*Then the LORD said,... 'You are not my people, and I am not your God'"* (Hosea 1:9). But He was still their rightful Lord, and His love for them would not let them go. *"How can I give you up?"* He said (Hosea 11:8).

Because they belonged to God, He delivered them time after time, from disaster after disaster. *"You will know that I, the Lord, am your Savior, your Redeemer, the Mighty One of Jacob,"* He said (Isaiah 60:16).

ADDICTED TO SIN

The world today desperately needs the Redemption of God, which does not give us up. All around us we can see how people turn away from God, even though they desperately need His love.

Money, military might, evil desires and selfishness are tyrannies that seem to rule everything. Many people are also driven by superstition and fear. In Africa, people who become Christians bring their witchcraft items and symbols to be burnt publicly.

But it is not only in Africa that people's lives are ruled by ungodly things. Millions throughout the world are ruled by the stars and spirits, or dominated by drugs and other addictions. While the men and women of the sports arena or the silver screen are idolised, God is forgotten. The Bible is speaking about us and the things we worship when it says: *"Here are your gods"* (1 Kings 12:28).

Millions hide from God as if He were their worst enemy. This is how it has been from the very beginning. God had to go searching in the Garden of Eden for Adam and Eve, calling, *"Adam, where are you?"* (Genesis 3:9). As the Bible says, *"We all, like sheep, have gone astray, each of us has turned to our own way"* (Isaiah 53:6).

Paul, in the New Testament, calls people *"the children of disobedience"* (Ephesians 2:2, KJV), who are in *"the trap of the devil, who has taken them captive to do his will"* (2 Timothy 2:26). Nothing has changed.

11

And he also says, *"Don't you know that when you offer yourselves to someone as obedient slaves, you are slaves of the one you obey—whether you are slaves to sin, which leads to death, or to obedience, which leads to righteousness?"* (Romans 6:16). Nobody can deny those Scriptures.

The Bible's picture of our world is of the strong man Samson who loved Delilah and fell asleep with his head on her lap while she treacherously plotted his destruction. The world is comfortable in the lap of the devil *"who has taken them captive to do his will"* (2 Timothy 2:26).

Each of us knows the bitterness of failure. Sin affects the way the whole world is run. It destroys nations, just as it destroyed Israel. Every news program proves it. Only bad news is news. If we started a list of our common evils, we would never finish it.

The Bible tells us about the terrible effects of all this: *"Your iniquities have separated you from your God"* (Isaiah 59:2). And it also asks one of the biggest questions that we can ever ask: *"How then can a mortal be righteous before God? How can one born of woman be pure?"* (Job 25:4).

HELP FROM OUTSIDE OURSELVES

The only answer in the world to this question is in the Bible. It is an answer that goes right to the heart of Redemption.

This is why Redemption is not about "going religious"—it is not as trivial as that. Instead, Redemption is as much a part of things as creation. The whole of human existence is poisoned by evil, but God has given us the antidote: Redemption by Jesus Christ. God never sold us out to the devil. He has ownership rights and responsibilities. He sent Jesus to begin the work of Redemption, and He will complete it.

Nobody can redeem themselves. Of course, some people think they can. They talk about living good, honest lives—but they still give God the cold shoulder. And when you think about it, a good honest slave is still a slave! He or she needs someone to set them free.

Or think of it in this way. We all blot our copybooks. If we turn over a new leaf, the old blotted leaves are still there. We need help to wipe away those blots—help that we cannot give ourselves. To redeem us cost Jesus the most awful effort—with grief, sweat, blood, tears ,and the agony of a public execution. If Jesus had to go through all this, how could you or I possibly redeem ourselves?

For thousands of years the heart of the human dilemma has been sin. We cannot free ourselves. We cannot make forgiveness for ourselves. And this is because sin goes right to the heart of us. The human heart, the Bible says, is *deceitful above all things, and desperately wicked*" (Jeremiah 17:9, NKJV).

No surgeon can operate and give us a sinless heart. No therapist can rid us of selfishness or hate. Science can do wonders, but science itself needs saving because it brings great evils as well as good. No computer could number our sins, or come up with a solution. The saints and the best people who ever lived shed hopeless tears over the evils of their own hearts.

But in the face of all this bad news, there is good news: Jesus saves!

SOMEONE WHO WAS "GOOD ENOUGH"

Think back for a moment to the story of the exodus. After four hundred years in Egypt, nobody was able to redeem the Israelites from their slavery. Moses was the greatest leader they ever had, but even he was not perfect. Later in the story, when Israel sinned and God spoke of blotting them all out, Moses offered his own life to ransom the nation. It was bluntly refused. Moses was simply not good enough to achieve redemption for his people.

There never was anyone good enough to stand before God and deliver the world. As the words of a famous Christian hymn say, "There was no other good enough to pay the price of sin."[3] The Bible is right when it says: *"There is no one righteous, not even one"* (Romans 3:10); *"All of us have become like one who is unclean, and all our righteous acts are like filthy rags"* (Isaiah 64:6).

No man or woman ever wore the jeweled crown of perfection—until the birth of a baby one night in Bethlehem: *"But when the time had fully come, God sent His Son, born of a woman, born under the law, to redeem those under law, that we might receive adoption to sonship"* (Galatians 4:4–5).

The Son of God became the Son of Man. He was the totally unselfish one, living every moment for us. And He was the one who was "good enough" to pay the price of sin.

THE ONE AND ONLY REDEEMER

There can never be a joint Redeemer, a co-Savior. It was Jesus Christ who came into the world for us, who suffered and died for us, and who was raised from the dead for us. Neither His foster father, Joseph, nor His mother, Mary, gave themselves for us. No apostle, no disciple, ever achieved what Jesus achieved for us. God is jealous of His rights as the Redeemer.

Only Jesus could achieve the work of Redemption, because He was not only a human being, but He was God Himself, living on earth. The Bible tells us that God the Father *"has rescued us from the dominion of darkness and brought us into the kingdom of the Son he loves, in whom we have redemption, the forgiveness of sins. The Son is the image of the invisible God, the firstborn over all creation"*

(Colossians 1:13–15).

---

[3] Cecil Frances Alexander, "There Is a Green Hill Far Away," Hymnary.org, accessed February 23, 2022

Despite this clear teaching, the false doctrine has been taught that Jesus was nothing but a human being, whom God exalted to sit beside Him. But no mere creature could ever become God to redeem us. God never became God, or He would not be God. God could not create another like Himself.

No creature can masquerade as the uncreated source of all things. No one can cross that gulf.

It was God—and not an angel—who breathed into Adam the breath of life. As the apostle Paul said, *"God...made the world and everything in it.... He himself gives everyone life and breath and everything else"* (Acts 17:24–25). Only God made us and owns us, and only God can redeem us.

The glorious truth is that while a human being cannot become God. God did become a human being in the person of Jesus Christ, so that He could redeem us. God says:

"I, even I, am the LORD, and apart from me there is no Savior. I am the LORD; that is my name! I will not give my glory to another. I, the LORD, am your Savior, your Redeemer." (Isaiah 43:11; 42:8; 49:26)

This is emphasized in chapter after chapter in the Book of Isaiah.

PAYING THE RANSOM

God redeemed Israel from Egypt, but when we talk about the eternal Redemption of Jesus Christ, there are some big differences. To begin with, the people of Israel were not redeemed from their sin, but only from Egypt. Because of their sins and faithlessness, they all died in the wilderness and only their children entered the land God had promised them. Then again, God gave no ransom, and Egypt got nothing for its hostages. God simply took what belonged to Him. It cost Him nothing, and He sent Israel away free. But for eternal Redemption, the payment was infinite.

The words of Jesus Himself give us an important key: *"The Son of Man did not come to be served, but to serve, and to give his life as a ransom for many"* (Mark 10:45). This is confirmed by the words of Paul: *"For there is one God and one mediator between God and mankind, the man Christ Jesus, who gave himself as a ransom for all"* (1 Timothy 2:5–6). A ransom is a price paid in exchange for a captive. It is the means of buying his or her freedom.

This does not mean that God paid a ransom into somebody's hands. But He did pay the price. The Son of God was not handed over to Satan in exchange for his captives. But God *"gave him up for us all"* (Romans 8:32). He surrendered Him into the hands of those who crucified Him. *"God so loved the world that he gave his one and only Son"* (John 3:16).

This was done not for a good world, but for a bad one. *"While we were still sinners, Christ died for us"* (Romans 5:8). He did not merely visit this world, but gave Himself for us in the most costly way. So that we could belong to Him, He belonged to us. *"Christ also suffered once for sins, the righteous for the unrighteous, to bring you to God"* (1 Peter 3:18).

PART 2

THE GREATEST LOVE STORY EVER TOLD

The Bible provides us with some moving illustrations of God's love for a lost world. Better than the best romantic novels, they show us His heartache, His utter devotion to us, and His practical solution. And the best thing of all is that it is real—not merely the stuff of fiction.

THE STORY OF HOSEA

Take, for example, the story of the prophet Hosea's redeeming love. He was a man who was honest and upright, and who was deeply committed to God. Despite this, the Lord told him to marry a wife who was unfaithful. In obedience to God, he did this. Hosea's wife bore children—but he was not their father. He named one of them "Lo-ammi"—which means "not my people."

Despite everything that Hosea did for her, his immoral wife sank lower and lower until she became a slave prostitute in a brothel.

Then God told Hosea to get her back, and more than that, to love her. So Hosea redeemed her, buying back his own wife for a handful of silver—fifteen shekels. He accepted her and loved her again. It was a picture of God's Redemption—a moving story of deep, self-sacrificing love.

The love of God is deeply offended by our sin and unfaithfulness, but the promise God gave to Hosea holds good for the whole world: *"I will deliver this people from the power of the grave; I will redeem them from death"* (Hosea 13:14). We can thank God for that. We see the hell that many people make of their own and other people's lives. Only God can put things right.

Hosea paid fifteen shekels to redeem his wife. But what were we worth to God? Peter, in the New Testament, tells us, *"For you know that it was not with perishable things such as silver or gold that you were redeemed from the empty way of life handed down to you from your ancestors, but with the precious blood of Christ, a lamb without blemish or defect"* (1 Peter 1:18–19).

THE STORY OF RUTH

Another story from the Bible gives us insight into a second aspect of Redemption—the role of the kinsman-redeemer.

In the Old Testament book of Ruth a man and his wife, Naomi, went with their two sons to live in the land of Moab. They were forced to make this journey, because there was famine in Israel. There the sons married. A few years later, both the sons and their father died, leaving behind three widows.

When Naomi heard that the famine in Israel was over, she decided to return to her homeland. The widow of one son stayed behind in Moab and went back to her parents. The other, Ruth, clung to her mother-in-law, and loyally refused to leave her. The two women made their way back into Israel, to Bethlehem.

Naomi had land rights there, and so did Ruth, as the widow of an Israeli man. Land in Israel was an inheritance that could never pass into the permanent ownership of another family. It could be leased, but not sold. If the land was forfeited through debt or any other circumstance, the original owner could still claim it back—in other words, he or she could redeem it.

This was all well and good, but Naomi and Ruth had no money to redeem the property. So it had to be done by a relative or kinsman who carried special family responsibilities. In the story of Ruth, a relation came forward called Boaz. But in order to reclaim the estate, Boaz would have to marry her. Now, Boaz had already been impressed by the self-sacrificing character of the young widow, and was willing to assume the full measure of his responsibilities. So, with the full blessing of the leaders of the town, he and Ruth married.

This was how a Moabite—a non-Jewish woman—became the great-grandmother of King David, and an ancestor of Jesus Christ.

OUR KINSMAN-REDEEMER

The story of Ruth gives us a picture of the great kinsman-redeemer, Jesus Christ. The human family needed a kinsman, a representative, to redeem our lost estate. Someone who was unrelated to us could not do it.

That is why the Bible stresses the humanity of Jesus as well as His divinity:

> *For to us a child is born, to us a son is given, and the government will be on his shoulders.... Of the increase of his government and peace there will be no end.*

(Isaiah 9:6–7)

We can find this in the New Testament, as well: *"Since the children have flesh and blood, he too shared in their humanity"* (Hebrews 2:14). Jesus, as a member of the human family, was the person God made responsible to redeem mankind's lost rights in the eternal scheme of God.

Actually, Israel certainly never thought of God as a kinsman. To them He seemed an awesome being, the wholly other One, holy and separate. He redeemed them simply by force, snatching them from under the nose of Pharaoh, with *"a mighty hand and an outstretched arm"* (Deuteronomy 26:8). Under His feet the Sinai mountain shivered and shook. *"He who is the Glory of Israel...is not a human being"* (1 Samuel 15:29).

But He who was *not a man* became man, our kinsman. The maker of human beings clothed Himself in the same flesh. How, we do not know—any more than we know how God made heaven and earth. It is a glorious mystery, but *"the Word became flesh and made his dwelling among us"* (John 1:14). He whom the heaven of heavens cannot contain became one of us on this planet.

He did more. *"Being in very nature God, he did not consider equality with God something to be used to his own advantage; rather...being found in appearance as a man, he humbled himself by becoming obedient to death—even death on a cross!"* (Philippians 2:6–8).

The value of Redemption must be judged by its price. *"Christ redeemed us...God sent his Son...to redeem those under the law"* (Galatians 3:13; 4:5). These verses of Paul use a special word for *redeem* which means "bought out of." Christ was our kinsman-redeemer when spiritually, like Ruth and Naomi, we were destitute. He secured our eternal inheritance and life with God. Nobody can take away what Jesus paid for on the cross.

THE DOWRY

In the East, when a young man saw a girl he wanted to marry, he first had to have his father's permission to seek her hand. Once his father had agreed, the young man went to the girl's home to ask for her father's consent to the marriage.

Next came the matter of the dowry. This was an amount of money, paid perhaps in silver or gold. The amount was settled by negotiation between the two families, and it formally established a legally binding marriage contract.

In this way, the couple became engaged. A year might go by before they married, but they both prepared for it. Then one night, in a torch-lit procession, the young man and his friends went over to the home of the bride, and formally "kidnapped" her—although she offered no resistance! They were then married, had a honeymoon, and everyone feasted. She was now the young man's *property*.

These customs are the background to a passage in one of the most famous letters of the New Testament: *"It was not with perishable things such as silver or gold that you were redeemed...but with the precious blood of Christ, a lamb without blemish or defect. He was chosen before the creation of the world"* (1 Peter 1:18–20).

THE ROYAL WEDDING

In the Bible, the company of those who are redeemed are described as "the bride of Christ". Just as in an Eastern wedding, God the Son came by the Father's will to the house of His bride—this world—to find those who would love Him.

And as in an Eastern wedding, the dowry was the vital issue. The Son paid with His precious blood, His own life. *"Christ loved the church and gave himself up for her to make her holy...to present her to Himself as a radiant church, without stain or wrinkle or any other blemish, but holy and blameless"* (Ephesians 5:25–27). No bride ever cost a bridegroom so much: *"the church of God, which he bought with his own blood"* (Acts 20:28). *"You are not your own; you were bought at a price"* (1 Corinthians 6:19–20).

There was no bargaining. The church was not a cheap bride. Jesus paid the full price. Joseph was sold for twenty silver shekels, and Judas sold Christ for thirty pieces of silver, but Christ gave everything, Himself, for us. What He did for us made everyone infinitely valuable. Jesus said that a single human soul was worth more than the whole world, and He meant it (Matthew 16:26). He gave all that He had for all that there were.

The payment of the dowry sealed the marriage contract. This is reflected in the Gospel. At the Last Supper, Jesus said, *"This cup is the new covenant in my blood, which is poured out for you"* (Luke 22:20). The marriage is arranged: hallelujah! That marriage contract cannot be annulled: *"Whoever comes to me I will never drive away"* (John 6:37).

Soon the Bridegroom will come like an Eastern bridegroom in His torch-lit procession. The coming of the Son of Man will be seen by everyone, and He will take away His bride. Then the marriage supper of the Lamb will take place.

There will be music and joy. Five times in the Book of Revelation we read of a new song. The old songs are the Psalms of Israel, but Jesus Christ has changed the worship and we sing, *"You...have redeemed us to God by your blood"* (Revelation 5:9, NKJV). The people of Israel sang about their redemption from Egypt. Christians sing of their Redemption from sin.

THE AVENGER

Not all the duties of a kinsman-redeemer were as pleasurable as those related in the story of Ruth and Boaz. In those cruel old days, he also had to be an avenger. If a man was killed, even accidentally, then the kinsman-redeemer had to avenge his death by slaying a man from the killer's family. The blood feud was a merciless, wicked practice that could go on between families for generations.

God hated this wickedness. In the Book of Judges (chapter 20) He commanded cities of refuge to be appointed for those who were fugitives. A man being pursued by an avenger could flee to a city of refuge. Once he was inside the gates, he was protected.

One example of a kinsman-redeemer avenging a life is found in the Book of Second Samuel (chapter 3). At that time, there was civil war in Israel, and Abner, the king's cousin, killed a man called Asahel. His brother Joab vowed vengeance. He feigned friendship with Abner and invited him to Hebron. They greeted one another outside the gates of the town, but there Joab treacherously stabbed Abner and he died.

The irony is that Hebron was a city of refuge. A few meters further and Abner would have been inside and safe. It became a saying: *"Abner [died] as a fool dies"* (2 Samuel 3:33, NKJV).

This grim story pictures the danger we are all in. Our sin will find us out. It will haunt us and hunt us even beyond the grave. Judgment is sure, like a pursuing vengeance. The Bible is clear about this: *"The soul who sins shell die"* (Ezekiel 18:4, NKJV); *"The wages of sin is death"* (Romans 6:23).

We need a city of refuge, a Redeemer. We read that God is *"patient with you, not wanting anyone to perish, but everyone to come to repentance"* (2 Peter 3:9). Our perfect hope is Jesus, because to repent and flee to Him brings us safety.

The New Testament often talks about being *"in Christ"*. Jesus said, *"Whoever comes to me I will never drive away"* (John 6:37). If we are not driven away, then we are invited in. Jesus is our city of refuge. As Paul says, *"Therefore, there is now no condemnation for those who are in Christ Jesus"* (Romans 8:1).

To die and not be in Christ is to die unredeemed, in unbelief and in our sins. It is to die *"as a fool dies "*—so near to safety, but foolishly outside the gates of mercy. There is only one place we can go to be saved:

> *The LORD is my rock, my fortress and my deliverer; my God is my rock, in whom I take refuge, my shield and the horn of my salvation, my stronghold. I called to the*

Lord, who is worthy of praise, and I have been saved from my enemies." (Psalm 18:2–3).

The greatest tragedy is to be unredeemed, when the Redeemer is so close at hand.

THE KINSMAN-REDEEMER
WHO DIED INSTEAD OF KILLING

Our Kinsman-Redeemer, Jesus, did a most wonderful thing. Wicked men had bound Him, lashed and crucified Him, the innocent One, unlawfully and unjustly. Should His death not be avenged? His followers might have attacked those who were guilty of this atrocity. Peter did strike one blow with his sword when Jesus was arrested, but Jesus told that quick-tempered man to put his sword away.

Jesus did not cry out for vengeance. Instead, as He was being nailed to the cross, He kept on praying: *"Father, forgive them"* (Luke 23:34).

Darkness then shrouded the scene, but from the heart of that blackness shone a bright ray of mercy and reconciliation. Paul expressed it in these words: *"God was reconciling the world to himself in Christ"* (2 Corinthians 5:19). *"God was pleased to have all his fullness dwell in him, and through him to reconcile to himself all things, whether things on earth or things in heaven, by making peace through his blood, shed on the cross"* (Colossians 1:19–20).

Whoever was guilty of Jesus' death, they were forgiven by His prayer, whether they were Greek, Roman, or Jewish. The blood of Jesus that they shed was their Redemption. Their pardon was handed to them at the very cross they erected. It was written by the pen of God dipped in the fountain of the precious blood of Jesus.

For centuries, the so-called "Christian" nations persecuted the Jewish people as "Christ killers." These "Christians" did not know God, the true account of His death, or the Scriptures. Their religion was corrupt. They were ignorant of its first principle of mercy. They had no idea about the wonderful spirit of forgiveness of the One they called their Savior and Redeemer. Christ forgave those who slew Him, and who is anybody else to take vengeance?

This was the wonderful thing which Jesus, our Kinsman-Redeemer, did. Instead of coming to avenge our sins, He allowed all the vengeance due to us to fall on Him. He became the great and ultimate victim, blocking the course of the blood-feud.

Sin pursued us, demanding the blood of the sinful. But Jesus offered His own blood to put an end to all vengeance. *"He himself is our peace, who has made the two groups one and has destroyed the barrier, the dividing wall of hostility. He came and preached peace to you who were far away and peace to those who were near"* (Ephesians 2:14, 17).

Peace! Joab slid a keen blade into Abner to take vengeance, but Jesus allowed His own body to receive a spear wound from those who hated Him. He accepted the shame of crucifixion in order to redeem us all. He proclaimed peace and forgiveness, not a "holy war" against the infidel. He comes to us with pity, not with punishment. His ministry is reconciliation.

When people are gripped by the demons of hate and violence, He is *"our great God and Savior, Jesus Christ, who gave himself for us to redeem us from all wickedness and to purify for himself a people that are his very own, eager to do what is good"* (Titus 2:13–14).

PRIVILEGE AND RESPONSIBILITY

They say that privilege brings responsibility. Paul once befriended a runaway slave called Onesimus. That young man became a Christian. Paul sent him back to his owner, Philemon, with a letter asking him to forgive Onesimus and take him back. Now the name Onesimus means "useful," and Paul made a pun on his name, saying that *"formerly he was useless to you, but now he has become useful both to you and to me"* (Philemon 11).

Redemption does not set us up and send us off to do our own thing. Instead, it brings us new responsibilities. *"You are not your own,"* says Paul. *"You were bought at a price. Therefore honor God with your bodies"* (1 Corinthians 6:19–20). *"You were bought at a price; do not become slaves of human beings"* (1 Corinthians 7:23). *"I urge you, brothers and sisters, in view of God's mercy, to offer your bodies as a living sacrifice, holy and pleasing to God—this is your true and proper worship"* (Romans 12:1).

Like Onesimus, we are to be useful, not useless. We are not redeemed merely in our own interests. God has a wider purpose.

Responsibility is a privilege. Earlier, we saw how Redemption can be pictured as a marriage. A man and woman take on new responsibilities when they marry each other, but those responsibilities are a pleasure and privilege. The redeemed have the responsibility to serve the One they belong to—what a privilege and joy!

On a sea journey to Rome, Paul once testified to the entire ship's company that God was the One *"to whom I belong and whom I serve"* (Acts 27:23). The Book of Revelation describes a countless multitude who have *"washed their robes and made them white in the blood of the Lamb. Therefore they are before the throne of God and serve him day and night"* (Revelation 7:14–15).

The *therefore* in this passage echoes the *therefore* in Romans chapter 12: "*Therefore...present your bodies a living sacrifice, holy, acceptable to God, which is your reasonable service*" (Romans 12:1, NKJV).

WITNESSES FOR GOD

Usefulness and service is one of God's promises to everyone who is redeemed. Life takes on direction and meaning. The reward for service is the privilege of greater service. If we serve God in small things, we will go on to serve Him in greater things, as Jesus said (Matthew 25:23).

What is our service? As Jesus said, "*You will be my witnesses*" (Acts 1:8).

Israel was redeemed not merely for their own sake, but to serve the whole world, to make known the name of the Lord. "*You are My witnesses, declares the Lord*" (Isaiah 43:10). But they missed their national purpose. The Lord came looking for fruit from His vineyard, but found none. They tried to keep God to themselves and deeply resented any suggestion that He cared for non-Jews. They believed that the only way for non-Jews to know God was to become proselyte Jews.

Christians must not make this same mistake of keeping God to themselves. History must not be repeated. Jesus said: "*You will be my witnesses ... to the ends of the earth*" (Acts 1:8). Could any responsibility be a greater privilege? Or more absorbing or satisfying? May we not repeat history and fail God!

PART 3

HOW CAN WE EXPERIENCE REDEMPTION?

FROM DEATH TO LIFE

What is the purpose of Redemption? It is to deliver us from our godless ways to begin a new way of life. We looked at this quotation from one of Paul's letters earlier, but it is worth thinking about it again now:

> *Jesus Christ...gave himself for us to redeem us from all wickedness and to purify for Himself a people that are His very own, eager to do what is good.* (Titus 2:13-14)

The purpose of Redemption is not fun, or a physical thrill, or tasting a supernatural experience. Most people live for the passing moment. Some people recite ritual chants as part of a quest for some kind of sensation, a feeling of inner tranquillity and comfort. But Jesus had a far greater aim when He gave His life for us. It was not to gratify us with some kind of mystical experience—a drug can do that! Instead, God wants to begin an eternal work in our lives—to redeem us—and to do it now.

At the beginning of the Bible, God showed His readiness to help His people when He redeemed Israel from Egypt, from its slavery and idols. The Bible has always proclaimed a redeeming God, waiting to deliver us from all that holds us down and keeps us back.

At the coming of Jesus, He took the initiative and stepped into the world arena to fight for human freedom. At the cross He gained for us eternal salvation and Redemption.

WHAT WE NEED TO DO

All that the people of Israel had to do to receive their redemption was to walk out of Egypt. God made that possible. They had a lamb for their last meal, put its blood in a basin and painted it on their doorways. Seeing this sign, the angel of destruction left them alone in the final plague of judgment on Egypt. This was the first Passover (Exodus 12).

We, too, need to be prepared to leave "Egypt"—to leave our old way of life, with its darkness, doubt, unbelief, godlessness, and sin. The contract that can set us free has already been signed, the ransom has been paid. We can know Redemption from everything in our past when we repent and believe the Gospel.

Christ is our Lamb of God. His precious blood was poured out so that we can be saved from destruction. This second Passover takes us from death to life: *"Whoever hears My word and believes him who sent me...has crossed over from death to life"* (John 5:24).

The Bible says, *"Everyone who calls on the name of the LORD will be saved"* (Joel 2:32). There is a prayer printed at the end of this book. If you have never called on God, asking Him for your Redemption, you can use it now. As you pray to God, believe in your heart, and join the company of the millions on earth and in heaven who are the redeemed of the Lord.

Dear Heavenly Father,

I respond to Your invitation and come to you in the name of Your Son, Jesus Christ.

I come with all my sins, heartaches, and addictions.

I turn away from evil and turn to You, Lord Jesus.

I put my faith in You alone.
You are the Son of the Living God.

I believe with my heart what I now confess with my mouth: You are my Savior, my Lord, and my God.

Thank You for having accepted me as your child. I open my self for Your Holy Spirit and will follow You all the days of my life. I believe You and receive You.

I pray in the name of Jesus.

Amen!

BONNKE.TV

Welcome to **BONNKE.TV** – the digital home of Reinhard Bonnke sermons, tv shows, and films.

From classic messages to the latest live streams, this is your one-stop, 24/7 outlet for Evangelist Bonnke's passionate, insightful, Spirit-led preaching and teaching.

And, of course, feel free to share this site with your friends, family... anyone you think will be blessed by Reinhard Bonnke's singular voice and mountain-moving faith.

BONNKE
CLASSICS

CFAN
TV SHOW

LEGACY

GODS
CALL

Evangelist
REINHARD BONN

RENEW YOUR FAITH

STREAMING 24/7

BE ENCOURAGED